COUNTRY

Formal Name: Syrian Arab Republic (Al Jumhuriyah al Arabiyah as Suriyah).

Short Form: Syria.

Term for Citizen(s): Syrian(s).

Capital: Damascus (population estimated at 5 million in 2004).

Other Major Cities: Aleppo (4.5 million), Homs (1.8 million), Hamah (1.6 million), Al Hasakah (1.3 million), Idlib (1.2 million), and Latakia (1 million).

Independence: Syrians celebrate their independence on April 17, known as Evacuation Day, in commemoration of the departure of French forces in 1946.

Public Holidays: Public holidays observed in Syria include New Year's Day (January 1); Revolution Day (March 8); Evacuation Day (April 17); Egypt's Revolution Day (July 23); Union of Syria, Egypt, and Libya (September 1); Martyrs' Day, to commemorate the public hanging of 21 dissidents in 1916 (May 6); the beginning of the 1973 October War (October 6); National Day (November 16); and Christmas Day (December 25). Religious feasts with movable dates include Eid al Adha, the Feast of the Sacrifice; Muharram, the Islamic New Year; Greek Orthodox Easter; Mouloud/Yum an Nabi, celebration of the birth of Muhammad; Leilat al Meiraj, Ascension of Muhammad; and Eid al Fitr, the end of Ramadan. In 2005 movable holidays will be celebrated as follows: Eid al Adha, January 21; Muharram, February 10; Greek Orthodox Easter, April 29–May 2; Mouloud, April 21; Leilat al Meiraj, September 2; and Eid al Fitr, November 4.

Flag:
The Syrian flag consists of three equal horizontal stripes of red, white, and black with two small green, five-pointed stars in the middle of the white stripe.

Click to Enlarge Image

HISTORICAL BACKGROUND

Present-day Syria is only a small portion of the ancient geographical Syrian landmass, a region situated at the eastern end of the Mediterranean Sea from which Western powers created the contemporary states of Syria, Lebanon, Jordan, and Israel in the post-Ottoman era of the early twentieth century. Greater Syria, as historians and political scientists often refer to this area, is a region connecting three continents, simultaneously cursed and blessed as a crossroads for commerce and a battleground for the political destinies of dynasties and empires. Exploited

1

politically, Greater Syria also has benefited immeasurably from the cultural diversity of the people who came to claim parts or all of it, and who remained to contribute to the remarkable spiritual and intellectual flowering that characterized Greater Syria's cultures in the ancient and medieval periods. Throughout history, Greater Syria has been the focal point of a continual dialectic, both intellectual and bellicose, between the Middle East and the West. Today, Syria remains an active participant in the trials and tribulations of a troubled and volatile region.

Early History: Since before 2000 BC, Syria has been an integral part of, or the seat of government for, powerful empires. The struggle among various indigenous groups as well as invading foreigners resulted in cultural enrichment and significant contributions to civilization, despite political upheaval or turmoil. The ancient city of Ebla existed at the center of an expansive empire around 2400 B.C. The chief site, unearthed in the vicinity of Aleppo in the 1970s, contained tablets providing evidence of a sophisticated and powerful indigenous Syrian empire that was involved with, and probably controlled, a vast commercial network linking Anatolia, Mesopotamia, Egypt, and the Aegean and Syrian coasts. The language of Ebla is believed to be the oldest Semitic language, and the extensive writings of the Ebla culture are proof of a brilliant culture that rivals those of the Mesopotamians and ancient Egyptians.

After the King of Akkad destroyed Ebla, Amorites ruled the region until their power was eclipsed in 1600 B.C. by the Egyptians. The following centuries saw Syria ruled by a succession of Canaanites, Phoenicians, Hebrews, Aramaeans, Assyrians, Babylonians, Persians, Greeks, Seleucids, Romans, Nabataeans, Byzantines, Muslim Arabs, European Christian Crusaders, Ottoman Turks, Western Allied forces, and the French. Although Syria has absorbed the legacies of these many and varied cultures, the very existence of this string of foreign dominating powers exemplifies the political, economic, and religious importance of Syria's strategic location.

Highlights of early Syrian history include the impact made by such dominant powers as the Phoenicians, Aramaeans, and Greek, Roman, and Byzantine Empires. During the second millennium B.C., the seafaring Phoenicians established a trade network among independent city-states and developed the alphabet. The Aramaeans, overland merchants who had settled in Greater Syria at the end of the thirteenth century B.C., opened trade to southwestern Asia, and their capital at Damascus became a city of immense wealth and influence. Aramaic ultimately displaced Hebrew as the vernacular in Greater Syria and became the language of commerce throughout the Middle East. Beginning in 333 B.C., with the conquest of the Persian Empire, Alexander the Great and his successors brought Western ideas and institutions to Syria. Following Alexander's death in 323 B.C., control of Greater Syria passed to the Seleucids, who ruled the Kingdom of Syria from their capital at Damascus for three centuries. In the first centuries A.D., Roman rule saw the advent of Christianity in Syria. Paul, considered to be the founder of Christianity as a distinct religion, was converted on the road to Damascus and established the first organized Christian Church at Antioch during the first century.

The Coming of Islam: Syria remained at the center of the new Christian religion until the seventh century, when the area succumbed to Muslim Arab rule. Prior to the Arab invasion, Byzantine oppression had catalyzed a Syrian intellectual and religious revolt, creating a Syrian national consciousness. The Muslim Arab conquest in A.D. 635 was perceived as a liberating force from the persecution of Byzantine rule, to which Syria had been subjected since A.D. 324.

But with Damascus as the seat of the Islamic Umayyad Empire, which extended as far as Spain and India between 661 and 750, most Syrians became Muslim, and Arabic replaced Aramaic. Syrian prestige and power declined after 750 when the Abbasids conquered the Umayyads and established a caliphate in Baghdad. Syria then became a mere province within an empire.

Muslim control of Christian holy places was elemental in provoking the first major Western colonial venture in the Middle East, when European Crusaders established the principalities of Edessa, Antioch, Tripoli, and the Latin Kingdom of Jerusalem between 1097 and 1144. The ensuing jihad against the foreign occupation was a unifying force for Arabs in Greater Syria until the area became a province of the Ottoman Empire in 1516. Syria's economy did not flourish under Ottoman rule, which lasted for 400 years. Yet, Syria continued to attract European traders and with them Western missionaries, teachers, scientists, and tourists whose governments began to agitate for certain rights in the region, including the right to protect Christians.

A Brief Period of Independence: The period between the outbreak of World War I in 1914 and the granting of France's mandate over Syria by the League of Nations in 1922 was marked by a complicated sequence of events during which Syrians achieved a brief period of independence (1919–20). However, three forces were at work against Arab nationalism: Britain's interest in keeping eastern Mesopotamia under its control in order to counter Russian influence and to protect British oil interests; the Jewish interest in Palestine; and France's determination to remain a power in the Middle East. Ultimately, Syria and Lebanon were placed under French influence, and Transjordan and Iraq, under British mandate. The termination of Syria's brief experience with independence left a lasting bitterness against the West and a deep-seated determination to reunite Arabs in one state. This quest was the primary basis for modern Arab nationalism.

The French Mandate: The period of French Mandate brought nearly every feature of Syrian life under French control. This oppressive atmosphere mobilized educated wealthy Muslims against the French. Among their grievances were the suppression of newspapers, political activity, and civil rights; the division of Greater Syria into multiple political units; and French reluctance to frame a constitution for Syria that would provide for eventual sovereignty, which the League of Nations had mandated. Only in the wake of a widespread revolt instigated by the Druze minority in 1925 did the French military government begin to move toward Syrian autonomy. Despite French opposition, the Soviet Union and the United States granted Syria and Lebanon recognition as sovereign states in 1944, with British recognition following a year later. These Allied nations pressured France to leave Syria, but it was not until a United Nations resolution in February 1946 ordering France to evacuate that Syrians finally attained sovereignty. By April 15, 1946, all French troops had left Syrian soil.

Independence: Syria endured decades of strife and turmoil as competing factions fought over control of the country's government following independence in 1946. This era was one of coups, countercoups, and intermittent civilian rule during which the army maintained a watchful presence in the background. From February 1958 to September 1961, Syria was joined with Egypt in the United Arab Republic (UAR). But growing Syrian dissatisfaction with Egyptian domination resulted in another military coup in Damascus, and Syria seceded from the UAR. Another period of instability ensued, with frequent changes of government. The Arab Socialist Resurrection (Baath) Party (hereafter, Baath Party), with a secular, socialist, Arab nationalist orientation, took decisive control in a March 1963 coup, often referred to as the Baath Revolution. The Baath Party had been active throughout the Middle East since the late 1940s, and a Baath coup had taken place in Iraq one month prior to the Baath take-over in Syria. Factionalism continued within the Baathist regime until the assumption of power by then-Minister of Defense Lieutenant General Hafiz al Assad following a bloodless military coup in November 1970. Internal conflict between the Baath Party's more moderate military wing and more extremist civilian wing had been exacerbated by external events, including Israel's defeat of the Syrians and Egyptians in the June 1967 war, as a result of which Syria lost territory in the Golan Heights, as well as Syria's disastrous intervention on behalf of the Palestine Liberation Organization (PLO) in Jordan in September 1970 (events later dubbed Black September).

Assad, approved as president by popular referendum in March 1971, quickly moved to establish an authoritarian regime with power concentrated in his own hands. His thirty-year presidency was characterized by a cult of personality, developed in order to maintain control over a potentially restive population and to provide cohesion and stability to government. The dominance of the Baath Party; the socialist structure of the government and economy; the military underpinning of the regime; the primacy of members of the Alawi sect, to which Asad belonged, in influential military and security positions; and the state of emergency imposed as a result of ongoing conflict with Israel further ensured the regime's stability. Nevertheless, this approach to government came at a cost. Dissent was harshly eliminated, the most extreme example being the brutal suppression in February 1982 of the Muslim Brotherhood, which objected to the state's secularism and the influence of the "heretical" Alawis. Moreover, the country's economy suffered, and progress was hindered by an overstaffed and inefficient public sector run overwhelmingly according to Baath Party dictates.

Hafiz al Assad died in 2000 and was promptly succeeded by his son, Bashar al Assad, after the constitution was amended to reduce the mandatory minimum age of the president from 40 to 34. Bashar was then nominated by the Baath Party and elected president in a popular referendum in which he ran unopposed. From the start, the younger Assad appeared to make economic and political reform a focus and a priority of his presidency. He has faced resistance from the old guard, however. After a brief period of relaxation and openness known as the Damascus Spring (July 2000–February 2001), dissent is once again not tolerated in Syria, and it appears that any reforms will be slow in coming. Nevertheless, Assad reportedly is slowly dismantling the old regime by enforcing mandatory retirement and replacing certain high-level administrators with appointments from outside the Baath Party.

GEOGRAPHY

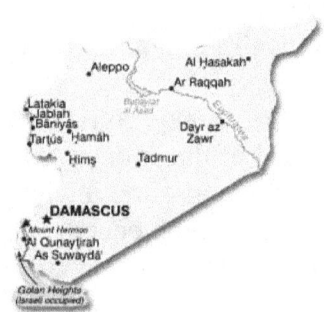

Location: Syria is located in southwestern Asia, at the eastern end of the Mediterranean Sea, with Turkey to the north, Iraq to the east, Jordan to the south, and Israel and Lebanon to the west.

Size: Syria is about the size of North Dakota, with a total land area of 185,180 square kilometers (184,050 square kilometers of land and

Click to Enlarge Image

4

1,130 square kilometers of water), including 1,295 square kilometers of Israeli-occupied territory.

Land Boundaries: Syria's land boundaries total 2,253 kilometers with the bordering nations of Iraq (605 kilometers), Israel (76 kilometers), Jordan (375 kilometers), Lebanon (375 kilometers), and Turkey (822 kilometers).

Disputed Territory: Territory disputed by Syria includes 1,295 square kilometers of the Golan Heights occupied by Israel in the 1967 Arab-Israeli War. A portion of the Golan Heights also is claimed by Lebanon. In addition, the Syrian government has never recognized the legality of Turkey's possession of Hatay Province, which was the Syrian province of Iskenderun until France ceded it to Turkey in 1939. Diversion of water from the Euphrates River for dams is a continuing source of conflict between Syria and both Turkey and Iraq.

Length of Coastline: Syria has 193 kilometers of coastline along the Mediterranean Sea.

Maritime Claims: Syria claims 12 nautical miles of territorial sea and a contiguous zone of 41 nautical miles.

Topography: In the west, a narrow coastal plain stretches south from the Turkish border to Lebanon. It is divided by a double band of mountains from the large eastern region, primarily a semiarid to arid plateau that encompasses mountain ranges, desert areas, and the Euphrates River basin. In the northwest, the Jabal an Nusayriyah mountain range, with peaks averaging 1,212 meters, runs parallel to the coastal plain, terminating just north of the Lebanese border. The Anti-Lebanon Mountains run south along the length of that border and have peaks of more than 2,700 meters. The Homs Gap, a small opening between the two mountain ranges, has served as a centuries-old trade and invasion route from the coast to the interior of the country. The high volcanic region of Jabal al Arab in the far south is the home of the country's Druze population. A low chain of mountains extending northeastward from the Jabal al Arab to the Euphrates River intersects Syria's expansive eastern plateau region. The barren desert region south of these mountains is called the Hamad. Northeast of the Euphrates River is the fertile Jazirah region.

Principal Rivers: The Euphrates River, originating in the mountains of Turkey and flowing diagonally southeastward across Syria into Iraq, is Syria's longest and most important river, providing 80 percent of Syria's water resources. Its left-bank tributaries, the Balikh and the Khabur, are both major rivers also originating in Turkey, but its right-bank tributaries are small seasonal streams called wadis. The Barada River, rising in the Anti-Lebanon Mountains in the southwest and disappearing into the desert, creates the Al Ghutah Oasis, the verdant site enabling Damascus to prosper since ancient times. In the northwest, the Orontes River irrigates the Al Ghab depression, a fertile, intermountain plateau region east of the coastal mountains.

Climate: The striking feature of the Syrian climate is the contrast between sea and desert. A semiarid steppe zone extends across about three-quarters of the country between the humid Mediterranean coast in the west and the arid desert regions to the south and east. The steppe experiences fairly abundant rainfall, with annual precipitation ranging between 750 and 1,000 millimeters, mostly falling between November and May. Annual mean temperatures range from

7.2° C in January to 26.6° C in August. The area east of the Anti-Lebanon Mountains, including Damascus, has precipitation averaging less than 200 millimeters a year and temperatures ranging from 4.4° C in January to 37.7° C in July and August.

Natural Resources: Syria has deposits of petroleum; natural gas; phosphates; chrome, iron, and manganese ores; asphalt; rock salt; marble; and gypsum. It also has hydropower resources, although operation of Syria's Euphrates Dam has been hampered by Turkey's diversion of water from the upper Euphrates for several dams of its own. Syria's use of the Euphrates in turn impedes water flow into Iraq.

Land Use: Depending on the source consulted, 25–32 percent of Syria's land area is classified as arable, and 4.4 percent was planted to permanent crops in 2001. An estimated 12,130 square kilometers were irrigated in 1998. The government has undertaken major irrigation projects in the north and northeast with the goal of increasing irrigated farmland from about 20 percent to more than 38 percent of the total in the coming decade.

Environmental Factors: Syria's major environmental issues include deforestation, overgrazing, soil erosion, desertification, water pollution from the dumping of raw sewage and wastes from petroleum refining, and inadequate supplies of potable water. Water shortages, exacerbated by population growth, industrial expansion, and water pollution, are a significant long-term constraint on economic development. Dust storms and sandstorms are natural hazards in desert areas.

Time Zone: Greenwich Mean Time plus two hours.

SOCIETY

Population: Syria's population was estimated at 18.2 million in July 2003 and was growing at an estimated rate of 2.4 percent in 2004. The annual growth rate from 1990–2002 was 2.6 percent. About 52 percent of the population was urban as of 2002, with a growth rate of 3.1 percent. Syria is one of the most densely populated countries in the Middle East (57 people per square kilometer in 1986 and about 363 per square kilometer in 2004), but there are significant regional variations. The population is concentrated along the coast in the west, in the south around Damascus, and in the Euphrates River Valley in the northeast. More than 400,000 Palestinian refugees are believed to reside in Syria. In addition, Syria has some 170,000 internally displaced people, mostly from the Golan Heights. An estimated 40,000 people remain in the Golan Heights, including about 20,000 Arabs and 20,000 Israeli settlers. In early 2005, news reports indicated that Syria had been "overwhelmed" by the influx of more than 700,000 Iraqis since the U.S.-led invasion of Iraq in 2003.

Demography: According to 2004 estimates, about 38 percent of Syrians are less than 15 years of age, 58.7 percent are 15–64 years of age, and 3.3 percent are 65 and older. The median age is 20 (19.9 for males and 20.2 for females). The sex ratio for the total population is 1.06 males per female. The birthrate in 2004 was estimated at 28.9 births per 1,000 and the total fertility rate at 3.6 children born per woman. The death rate in 2004 was estimated at nearly 5 deaths per 1,000.

Estimated life expectancy at birth was 69.7 years for the total population (68.5 for males and 71.0 for females). According to UNICEF, the infant mortality rate for 2002 was 23 per 1,000, significantly down from the rate of 136 per 1,000 in 1960, but the U.S. government estimated the infant mortality rate at 30.6 per 1,000 in 2004.

Ethnic Group(s): Approximately 90 percent of Syrians are Arabs, and about 9 percent are Kurds. Armenians, Circassians, and Turkomans make up the remaining 1 percent of the population.

Languages: Arabic is the official language and mother tongue of about 90 percent of the population. Minority languages include Kurdish, Armenian, Aramaic, and Circassian. Both English and French are widely understood, especially by educated elites in major urban areas.

Religion: The majority of Syrians are Sunni Muslims, comprising 74 percent of the population. Minority religious groups include Alawis, a heterodox Shia Muslim sect (12 percent); Christians (10 percent); Druze, a religious group located in southern Syria whose beliefs contain elements of Shia Islam, Christianity, and paganism (3 percent); and small numbers of other Muslim sects, Jews (who have tiny communities in Damascus, Al Qamishli, and Aleppo), and Yazidis (a small religious group whose religion contains elements of Islam, Judaism, and Christainity).

Education and Literacy: Despite being a low-income country with a growing population, Syria has a good basic education system. The Baath Party promotes the idea that education is one of the foundations of economic development. Syria's literacy rate of 60 percent for men and 50 percent for women, according to one estimate, is higher than Egypt's but lower than that of Jordan or Lebanon. Other sources cite a literacy rate of 76.9 percent total, 89.7 percent for men and 64 percent for women, in 2003. Most education is state provided, but legislation passed in 2001 allows the establishment of some private schools and colleges. Resources for education have risen in absolute terms over the past decade, but it is difficult to match the rate of population growth. Showing an increase over 2002 spending, 8.6 percent of the state budget was earmarked for education in 2003.

Six years of primary school for children ages 6–11 are free and compulsory, and enrollment is near 100 percent for both boys and girls. At the secondary level, the education system also includes three years of general or vocational education followed by three years of academic or vocational education. However, classes are large and facilities poor at all levels. Domestic policies emphasize engineering and medicine in Syria's four universities, with less emphasis on the arts, law, and business. In September 2002, the president founded the country's first virtual university through which students can obtain degrees from U.S. institutions. This measure and others, such as making computer literacy mandatory at the high-school level and English- and French-language instruction compulsory in the elementary schools, have the goal of equipping students with computer and language skills in order to modernize the economy through the education system.

Health: The Baath Party has placed an emphasis on health care, but funding levels have not been able to keep up with demand or maintain quality. Health expenditures reportedly accounted for 2.5 percent of the gross domestic product (GDP) in 2001. Syria's health system is relatively decentralized and focuses on offering primary health care at three levels: village, district, and provincial. According to the World Health Organization (WHO), in 1990 Syria had 41 general hospitals (33 public, 8 private), 152 specialized hospitals (16 public, 136 private), 391 rural health centers, 151 urban health centers, 79 rural health units, and 49 specialized health centers; hospital beds totaled 13,164 (77 percent public, 23 percent private), or 11 beds per 10,000 inhabitants. The number of state hospital beds reportedly fell between 1995 and 2001, while the population had an 18 percent increase, but the opening of new hospitals in 2002 caused the number of hospital beds to double. WHO reported that in 1989 Syria had a total of 10,114 physicians, 3,362 dentists, and 14,816 nurses and midwives; in 1995 the rate of health professionals per 10,000 inhabitants was 10.9 physicians, 5.6 dentists, and 21.2 nurses and midwives. Despite overall improvements, Syria's health system exhibits significant regional disparities in the availability of health care, especially between urban and rural areas. The number of private hospitals and doctors increased by 41 percent between 1995 and 2001 as a result of growing demand and growing wealth in a small sector of society. Almost all private health facilities are located in large urban areas such as Damascus, Aleppo, Tartus, and Latakia.

Key health indicators in Syria show that infectious diseases and illnesses related to environmental pollution remain serious problems. The rate of prevalence of human immunodeficiency virus/acquired immune deficiency syndrome (HIV/AIDS) in 2001 was 0.01 percent. About 80 percent of Syrians had access to water in 2000 and 90 percent to sanitation.

Welfare: Syria's socialist government provides extensive social services to citizens at nominal cost. Most welfare programs are administered by the ministry of Social Affairs and Labor, which also controls labor unions, sets the minimum wage, regulates safety, pays social security, and operates orphanages, institutions for the handicapped, and rural community development centers. Many citizens have access to subsidized public housing, and many basic commodities are heavily subsidized.

ECONOMY

Overview: Syria had a relatively well-developed agricultural and industrial base at independence in 1946, but following independence the economy underwent widespread structural change. When the Baath Party became the major political force in the 1960s, Syria's economic orientation and development strategy were transformed. Government-sponsored land reform and the nationalization of major industries and foreign investments confirmed the socialist direction of the country's economic policy. With the high oil prices of the 1970s, Syria experienced a shift away from the traditional agrarian base to an economy dominated by the services, industrial, and commercial sectors, but a series of crises in the 1980s caused the economic climate to shift again, this time from prosperity to austerity. The government instituted limited reforms to respond to the burgeoning crisis, but the pressing economic problems required a radically restructured economic policy in order to improve performance. The principal challenge of reform is to modernize and transform an inefficient centralized economy.

Unlike many of its Arab neighbors, Syria has a diversified economy that is not overly dependent on oil. However, economic development has been hampered by a number of internal and external factors and has not kept pace with population growth. Historical problems affecting economic growth in Syria include a preoccupation with the Israeli threat and an obsession with internal order; massive defense and security spending has taken precedence over economic reform. Additionally, the overstaffed and inefficient public sector of the predominantly statist economic system has drained the economy by soaking up government expenditures and foreign exchange. Modest reforms are beginning to have a positive impact, and some sectors that were exclusively state-operated have opened to private-sector participation and foreign investment. New investment laws have encouraged private-sector growth by gradually expanding the list of goods that the private sector may produce or import and have permitted private competition with the government in some areas, such as textile and pharmaceutical manufacturing. However, the government continues to control strategic industries, such as oil production and refining, telecommunications, air transport, power generation and distribution, and water distribution, as well as the price of key agricultural goods. Moreover, resistance from senior regime members, entrenched interests, and a bureaucracy staffed with unskilled workers has hampered the reform effort. Assad remains committed to reform, but the effort is not comprehensive or integrated.

Gross Domestic Product (GDP): World Bank estimates place the total GDP for 2003 at US$21.5 billion, up from US$19.9 billion in 2002. The World Bank measured Syria's GDP growth at 2.5 percent in 2003, down from 3.2 percent in 2002. A U.S. government estimate of Syria's GDP growth was 3.5 percent in 2001 and 4.5 percent in 2002. GDP per capita was estimated to be US$1,165 in 2003. The agriculture sector historically accounted for the largest share of GDP, but it has been displaced by services and by mining and manufacturing. In 2003 agriculture accounted for 28.5 percent of GDP, industry for 29.4 percent, and services for 42.1 percent.

Government Budget: In 2004 government revenues were estimated at US$6.1 billion and expenditures at US$7.4 billion, including capital expenditures of US$3.6 billion. Public debt was equivalent to 89 percent of gross domestic product (GDP).

Inflation: Consumer price inflation was estimated to be 1.5 percent in 2004.

Agriculture: Agriculture is a high priority in Syria's economic development plans, as the government seeks to achieve food self-sufficiency, increase export earnings, and halt rural out-migration. The agriculture sector generates more than 25 percent of the national income and employs about 30 percent of the labor force. Agriculture constituted 28.5 percent of GDP in 2003 and 25 percent of nominal output in 2002, of which livestock accounted for 16 percent and fruit and grains for more than 40 percent. Most land is privately owned, a crucial factor behind the sector's success. About 28 percent of Syria's land area is cultivated, and 21 percent of that total is irrigated. Most irrigated land is designated "strategic," meaning that it encounters significant state intervention in terms of pricing, subsidies, and marketing controls. "Strategic" products such as wheat, barley, and sugar beets, must be sold to state marketing boards at fixed prices, often above world prices in order to support farmers, but at a significant cost to the state budget. The most widely grown arable crop is wheat, but the most important cash crop is cotton; cotton was the largest single export before the development of the oil sector. Nevertheless, the total area planted with cotton has declined because of an increasing problem of water shortage coupled with old and inefficient irrigation techniques. The output of grains like wheat is often underutilized because of poor storage facilities.

Forestry: Less than 3 percent of Syria's land area is forested, and only a portion of that is commercially useful. Limited forestry activity is centered in the higher elevations of the mountains just inland from the coast, where rainfall is more abundant.

Mining and Minerals: Phosphates are the major minerals exploited in Syria. Production dropped sharply in the early 1990s when world demand and prices fell, but output has since increased to more than 2 million tons in 2001. Marble, gypsum, stone, salt, gravel, and sands are also produced but generally not for export.

Industry and Manufacturing: The industrial sector, which includes mining, manufacturing, construction, and petroleum, accounted for 29.4 percent of gross domestic product (GDP) in 2003 and employed about 30 percent of the labor force. The main industrial products are petroleum, textiles, processed food, beverages, tobacco, and phosphates. Syria's manufacturing sector was largely state dominated until the 1990s, when economic reforms allowed greater local and foreign private-sector participation. Private participation remains constrained, however, by the lack of investment funds, input/output pricing limits, cumbersome customs and foreign exchange regulations, and poor marketing.

Because land prices are not controlled by the state, real estate is one of the few domestic avenues for investment with realistic and safe returns. Activity in the construction sector tends to mirror changes in the economy. Investment Law No. 10 of 1991, which opened the country to foreign investment in some areas, marked the beginning of a strong revival, with growth in real terms increasing over 2001 and 2002.

Energy: In 2001 Syria reportedly produced 23.3 billion kWh of electricity and consumed 21.6 billion kWh. As of January 2002, Syria's total installed electric generating capacity was 7.6 GW, with fuel oil and natural gas serving as the primary energy sources and 1.5 GW generated by hydroelectric power. A network totaling 45 GW linking the electric power grids of Syria, Egypt, and Jordan was completed in March 2001. Syria's electric supply capacity is an important national priority, and the government hopes to add 3,000 MW of power generating capacity by 2010 at a probable cost of US$2 billion, but progress has been slowed by a lack of investment capital. Power plants in Syria are undergoing intensive maintenance, and four new generating plants have been built. The power distribution network has serious problems, with transmission losses estimated as high as 25 percent of total generated capacity as a result of poor quality wires and transformer stations. A project for the expansion and upgrading of the power transmission network is scheduled for completion in 2005.

The first commercial oil field began production in 1968, but Syria did not begin exporting oil until the mid-1980s. Although Syria is not a major oil exporter by Middle Eastern standards, oil is a major pillar of the economy. Exact oil output levels are difficult to obtain, but according to one U.S. government estimate, Syria produced 522,700 barrels per day (bbl/d) in 2004 and consumed 265,000 bbl/d in 2001. The oil sector of the economy faces many challenges, such as a decline in output and production resulting from technological problems and a depletion of oil reserves. Reserves reportedly peaked at 590,000 bbl/d in 1996 and have fallen to 535,000 bbl/d in 2003 or a total of 2.4 billion barrels in 2004. Since older fields have reached maturity, oil production is expected to continue its decline. Meanwhile, consumption is rising, which means that Syria could become a net oil importer within a decade. To counteract this problem, Syria has intensified oil exploration efforts. Another option is switching electric power plants from oil-fired to natural gas-fired. Proven natural gas reserves, approximately three-quarters of which are owned by the Syrian Petroleum Company, were estimated at 240.7 billion cubic meters in 2004. The primary challenge for the natural gas industry is logistics: reserves are located mainly in northeastern Syria, whereas the population is concentrated in the west and south. In 2001 Syria reportedly both produced and consumed 5.8 million cubic meters of natural gas. Several projects are underway to increase natural gas production, including an onshore pipeline network connecting Egypt, Jordan, Lebanon, and Syria.

Services: Services accounted for 42.1 percent of gross domestic product (GDP) in 2003 and employed 39.7 percent of the labor force (including government) in 2002.

Banking and Finance: The financial services sector is nationalized. Six specialized state banks (the Central Bank of Syria, Commercial Bank of Syria, Agricultural Co-Operative Bank, Industrial Bank, Popular Credit Bank, and Real Estate Bank) each extend funds to, and take deposits from, a particular sector. The Central Bank of Syria controls all foreign exchange and trade transactions and gives priority to lending to the public sector. The Industrial Bank also is directed more toward the public sector and is undercapitalized. As a result, the private sector often is forced to bank abroad, a process that is more expensive and therefore a poor solution to industrial financing needs. Many businesspeople travel abroad to deposit or borrow funds. It is estimated that Syrians have deposited US$6 billion in Lebanese banks. The U.S. sanctions of May 2004 may increase the role of Lebanese and European banks because a ban on transactions between U.S. financial institutions and the Central Bank of Syria will create an increase in demand for intermediary sources for U.S. dollar transfers.

Syria has no investment banks, private insurance companies, or foreign banks, although five foreign banks were given licenses in December 2002, in compliance with Law 28 of March 2001, which allows the establishment of private and joint-venture banks. Foreigners are allowed up to 49 percent ownership of a bank, but may not hold a controlling stake. It is unclear what range of services private banks will be allowed to offer or what impact they may have on the demand for financial services. Syria has no equity or official currency markets. Legislation was passed in 2001 to establish a stock market, but the necessary regulatory and structural requirements are currently inadequate.

Tourism: The number of non-Arab visitors to Syria has doubled since the 1990s to 1.1 million in 2002, but this figure includes all visitors to the country, not just tourists. The total number of Arab visitors in 2002 was 3.2 million, most coming from Lebanon, Jordan, Saudi Arabia, and Iraq. Many Iraqi businesspeople set up ventures in Syrian ports to run import operations for Iraq, causing an increased number of Iraqis visiting Syria in 2003–4. Tourism is a potentially large foreign exchange earner and a source of economic growth. Tourism generated more than 6 percent of Syria's gross domestic product in 2000, and more reforms are being discussed to increase tourism revenues. As a result of projects derived from Investment Law No. 10 of 1991, hotel bed numbers had increased 51 percent by 1999 and increased further in 2001. A plan was announced in 2002 to develop ecological tourism with visits to desert and nature preserves. Two new luxury hotels are scheduled to open in Damascus at the end of 2004.

Labor: In 2004 the Syrian labor force was estimated to total about 5 million. An estimated 39.7 percent worked in the services sector (including government), 30.3 percent in agriculture, and 30 percent in industry and commerce in 2002. About 70 percent of Syria's workforce earns less than US$100 per month. Unemployment in Syria increased in the second half of the 1990s, and unofficial estimates put the figure at more than 20 percent in 2002. Anecdotal evidence suggests that many more Syrians are seeking work over the border in Lebanon than official numbers indicate. Each year more than 200,000 new job seekers enter the Syrian job market, but the economy has not been able to absorb them. In 2002 the Unemployment Commission (UC) was established, tasked with creating several hundred thousand jobs over a five-year period.

Foreign Economic Relations: Syria has good trade relations with neighboring Arab countries and enjoys free-trade arrangements with Algeria, Bahrain, Egypt, Kuwait, Libya, Morocco, Oman, Qatar, Sudan, and Tunisia as part of the Greater Arab Free Trade Area (GAFTA). Syria applies strict enforcement of the Arab League boycott of Israel, which is frequently a hindrance to trade. In late 2001, Syria submitted a formal request to join the World Trade Organization (WTO), having withdrawn from the WTO's predecessor, the General Agreement on Tariffs and Trade, in 1951 to protest Israel's membership. However, Syria will have to make significant changes in its current trade rules in order to qualify for WTO membership. Syria also is eager to enter into association with the European Union. Trade relations with the United States have been disrupted by the U.S. imposition of sanctions against Syria in mid-2005.

Imports: Imports in 2003 totaled an estimated US$4.8 billion free on board. The main commodities imported were machinery and transport equipment, electric power machinery, food and livestock, metal and metal products, chemicals and chemical products, plastics, yarn, and paper. The primary sources of imports were Germany (7.2 percent), Italy (7.1 percent), China (6.3 percent), France (5.9 percent), and Turkey (5.4 percent). Syrian imports accounted for 7.2 percent of the gross domestic product in 2003, down from 29.5 percent in 2002.

Exports: Exports in 2003 totaled an estimated US$5.1 billion free on board. The principal commodities exported were crude oil, petroleum products, phosphates, fruits and vegetables, cotton fiber, clothing, meat and live animals, and wheat. The main recipients of exports were Germany (20.9 percent), Italy (12.6 percent), the United Arab Emirates (7.6 percent), Lebanon (6.2 percent), Turkey (6 percent), France (5.4 percent), Croatia (4.8 percent), and the United States (4.1 percent). Syrian exports accounted for 7.4 percent of the gross domestic product in 2003, down from 38.3 percent in 2002.

Trade Balance: In 2003 Syria had an estimated trade balance of US$300 million.

Balance of Payments: The official data for the Syrian economy are unreliable because of significant and contradictory revisions to the official statistics by the Central Bank of Syria. However, certain trends can be discerned. A surplus was possible during the period of 1999–2001 because of an upward trend in world oil prices and some recovery in Syria's agricultural exports. A surplus was also possible between 2001 and 2002 because of a surplus in visible goods trade and a surge in trade with Iraq. Between 2001 and 2003, Syria imported Iraqi crude oil at a discount for domestic use, which freed up Syrian crude for export and added significantly to Syria's foreign reserves. However, a deficit in the balance of payments is likely for 2003 as a result of the cutoff of trade and oil flows from Iraq. In 2003 the current account was estimated at –US$72 million. Foreign exchange and gold reserves were estimated at US$3.3 billion in 2004. Remittances from workers abroad and foreign aid traditionally cover Syria's budgetary and trade deficits.

External Debt: In 2004 Syria's estimated external debt totaled US$21.6 billion. Syria is seeking to reschedule its bilateral debt, but a huge outstanding debt to the former Soviet Union remains a serious issue.

Foreign Investment: Figures on foreign direct investment in Syria are not available. However, despite recent reforms, Syria's state-controlled economy is not conducive to foreign investment. The problem is exacerbated by the lack of access to international money and capital markets for investors.

Foreign Aid: In 1997 foreign aid totaled an estimated US$199 million. The World Bank reported that as of July 2004 it had committed a total of US$661 million for 20 operations in Syria. One investment project remained active at that time.

Currency and Exchange Rate: Syria's currency is the Syrian pound (SP or SYP), equal to 100 piastres. The Syrian pound is pegged to the U.S. dollar and trades at both official and free-market rates. According to the Central Bank of Syria, the official exchange rate has been SP11.20–11.25 per US$1 since 1998; in early 2005, the bank gave the prevailing "neighboring markets rate" as SP46.0–SP46.5 per US$1. Other sources cited a free-market rate of SP51.91 to US$1 in early April 2005.

Fiscal Year: Calendar year.

TRANSPORTATION AND TELECOMMUNICATIONS

Overview: Since independence, the state has sought to develop a national transportation system connecting major population and economic areas, and improvements to infrastructure have figured prominently in economic development plans. The telecommunications system has been characterized as reasonably good and undergoing major improvements, including digital upgrades and fiber-optic technology. The current regime has placed great emphasis on enhancing Iraq's Internet access.

Roads: Syria has an extensive and reasonably well-maintained network of 23,400 kilometers of main roads and 18,400 kilometers of secondary roads connecting major cities and linking to neighboring countries. About 10,000 kilometers of roads were reported to be paved, including almost 900 kilometers of expressways, as of 1999. A Kuwaiti company has undertaken a major road improvement project of upgrading the roadway between Latakia and Aleppo. The number of vehicles also has grown steadily with the decline in import duties on cars. A portion of the rapid expansion stems from the increase in Japanese- and Korean-made minibuses, which serve as privately owned and operated transport systems. This expansion in road transport comes at the expense of the rail network, however.

Railroads: Syria's 2,425-kilometer rail network (standard-gauge) is generally adequate for transport needs. A recently initiated project is designed to upgrade the overall rail system and to improve links with neighboring countries, but the effort has been hampered between Damascus and Amman, Jordan, because a portion of the track in that area is narrow gauge. There is inexpensive, regular, but infrequent passenger service from Syria to Jordan, Turkey, Iran, and Iraq. Because of an increase in the speed and cost effectiveness of road transport, the rail system has experienced a decline in passengers, although the decline has been partly offset by a steady increase in freight use, especially for bulk commodities such as petroleum products, phosphates, cereals, and cement. In 1998, the last year for which statistics are available, Syrian trains recorded 182 million passenger-kilometers and carried about 5 million tons of freight. Syrian Railways is currently negotiating the purchase of 41 new locomotives.

Ports: Syria's main ports are located at Baniyas, Jablah, Latakia, and Tartus. Tartus and Latakia each service approximately 2,800 vessels per year, with 1.5 million tons of goods loaded and 6.9 million tons of goods unloaded. Latakia handles primarily general cargo and Tartus, both general cargo and phosphates. Baniyas primarily serves the oil industry. Port facilities in both Tartus and Latakia need equipment upgrades. The European Investment Bank recently signed a loan agreement to finance the development and modernization of the Tartus port, and Russian and Greek companies are conducting a dredging project to enable larger ships to anchor at both ports. Ports are state-run and lack sufficient funding; inadequate facilities, slow turnaround, cumbersome customs processing and regulations, and abundant corruption hamper port operations. The Ministry of Transport has attempted to lower fees in order to make Syrian ports more competitive with neighboring country ports, but shippers reportedly still find them outdated and inefficient.

In 2003 Syria's merchant marine totaled 122 ships: 12 bulk, 101 cargo, 2 container, 4 livestock carrier, 1 petroleum tanker, 1 refrigerated cargo, and 1 roll on/roll off. Fifteen vessels are foreign owned, and 83 are registered in other countries.

Inland Waterways: Approximately 900 kilometers of inland waterways in Syria are navigable, but this method of transport is not regarded as economically significant.

Civil Aviation and Airports: In 2003 Syria had a reported 93 airports, including 26 with paved runways and five with runways of more than 3,000 meters, as well as seven heliports. Syria's three international airports, located at Damascus, Aleppo, and Latakia, carry an average of 2.5 million passengers on 13,000 flights each year. Syria also moved 33,000 tons of freight by air in 2001. The government-owned national carrier, Syrian Arab Airlines (SyrAir) offers scheduled services to destinations throughout the Middle and Far East, Europe, and North Africa. SyrAir completed a major upgrade of its fleet in early 2000 when it received the last of the six A-320 Airbus aircraft it had purchased. SyrAir also released tenders to overhaul its aging Boeing aircraft. The remainder of the fleet is mostly Soviet-era aircraft used for domestic travel.

Pipelines: Syria had 2,300 kilometers of gas pipelines and 2,183 kilometers of oil pipelines in 2004. Syria lost a major source of revenue in March 2003 when the war in Iraq shut down a pipeline carrying crude oil into Syria.

Telecommunications: Telecommunications, which are controlled by the Syrian Telecommunications Establishment and regulated by the Ministry of Communications, are developing steadily despite limited resources. The government has given priority to the improvement of telecommunications and has used development funds from Gulf states to install modern digital systems throughout the country. Telephone lines increased from 500,000 in 1991 to about 2 million in 2002, but fell well short of the government's goal of 3.4 million lines by 2002 and 4 million by 2004. The waiting list for main lines is reported to exceed 2 million lines. Teledensity was only 14.7 per 100 in 2002, ranking Syria fifth lowest in the Middle East region; the government was aiming for a teledensity of 10 per 100 by 2004. Syria has not kept pace with the rest of the region in developing its mobile telecommunications network. In early 2001, the government issued two build-operator-transfer (BOT) telephone licenses for the installation of a mobile communications network involving 850,000 lines. The two companies involved had previously created limited pilot service in Damascus and Aleppo beginning in early 2000. The mobile network had reached a capacity of 60,000 by mid-2001 and was being expanded, reaching about 400,000 cell phones by 2002.

Syria is reported to have 44 TV stations and 14 AM and 2 FM radio broadcast stations. Since establishing a government Internet service provider (ISP) in 1997 (the Syrian Telecommunications Establishment), Syria has been opening to the Internet, and Internet and e-mail access, although still limited, are growing. Two state-owned ISPs now exist, but subscriptions are restricted to state institutions, public-sector companies, and the offices of selected professionals (such as doctors, lawyers, and journalists). With high installation, subscription, and hourly access fees, the costs are prohibitive. Syria has one of the lowest Internet penetration rates in the region, with only 250,000 subscribers in the early 2000s. However, the number of users may be much higher than the number of subscribers, given the recent proliferation of Internet cafés in the main cities and the fact that some Syrians are connected to the Internet via ISPs in neighboring countries. With the eventual advent of privately owned ISPs, Internet access rates should increase, thus meeting one of the goals of President Assad's modernization campaign. Additionally, he would like to raise the number of personal computers in the country, currently estimated to number only one computer per 56 people.

GOVERNMENT AND POLITICS

Government Overview: Ostensibly a republic, in reality Syria is an authoritarian, military-dominated regime where opposition to the president is not tolerated, and, with the succession of the previous president's son, concern about hereditary rule is plausible. Whereas the citizens may vote for the president and members of parliament, they cannot change the government; the president, for example, is not actually elected but, rather, confirmed by unopposed popular referenda. Parliament may assess and sometimes modify laws proposed by the executive branch, but it may not initiate laws. The president and his senior aides make most decisions in the political, economic, and security sectors, with a very limited degree of public accountability. The regime does not tolerate political opposition and justifies itself by maintaining a state of emergency that has been in effect since 1963 as a result of the state of war that continues to exist with Israel.

With the constitution ceding primacy to the Arab Socialist Resurrection (Baath) Party, all three branches of government are dominated by its views. The party is both socialist (advocating state ownership of the means of industrial production and redistribution of agricultural land) and revolutionary (espousing the goal of carrying the socialist revolution to every part of the Arab world). However, since August 1990 the regime has de-emphasized the socialist aspect in favor of pursuing pan-Arab unity. The regime's survival hinges on its strong desire for stability and its success in giving groups such as religious minorities and peasant farmers a stake in society. Perhaps more important, the expansion of government bureaucracy has created a large class of citizens loyal to the regime. The army and internal security apparatus, the units most responsible for enforcing the regime's stability, are loyal, effective, and dominated by the Alawi sect, to which the Assad family belongs.

Following the death of Hafiz al Assad in 2000, his son Bashar was nominated and confirmed as president. Bashar al Assad is a reform-minded president, and although his reforms have been met with resistance from the old guard, the country appears to have the potential for some modification of its system of government. There reportedly have been calls to make the Baath Party less influential in government and speculation that the president might push to remove the article of the constitution granting the party primacy.

Constitution: Syria's Permanent Constitution of March 13, 1973, provides for a republican form of government described as "a democratic, popular, socialist, and sovereign state." The constitution stipulates that the president must be a Muslim, and the main source of legislation must be Islamic doctrine and jurisprudence, although Islam is not specifically designated as the state religion. The Baath Party is named "the vanguard party in the society and the state." Governmental powers are divided among executive, legislative, and judicial branches, but the already formidable role of the presidency is strengthened by the constitution. Economic principles set forth a planned socialist economy. The constitution also reaffirms the ideological promise that Syria is only part of the one and indivisible "Arab nation" that is struggling for complete Arab unity.

Branches of Government: In the executive branch, the president is approved by unopposed popular referendum for a renewable seven-year term. According to the constitution, the candidate must be a Syrian Arab Muslim, proposed by the Baath Party, and nominated by the legislature. The constitution was amended in June 2000 to reduce the mandatory minimum age of the president from 40 to 34 in order to make Hafiz al Asad's son, Bashar, eligible for nomination. The president can be removed from power only in the case of committing high treason. He is both head of state and chief executive officer of the government as well as commander in chief of the armed forces. He appoints his vice presidents (two), appoints and dismisses the prime minister, deputy prime ministers, and other members of the Council of Ministers (the cabinet), as well as military officers. The Council of Ministers serves collectively as the executive and administrative arm of the president and the state. The president holds the right to dissolve the legislature. Other presidential prerogatives include the right to declare war and a state of emergency, issue laws to be ratified by the People's Council, declare amnesty, and approve five-year economic plans.

The legislative branch consists of a 250-seat unicameral People's Council. Members are elected by direct popular vote on the basis of single-member electoral districts for four-year terms. Half of the seats in the People's Council are reserved for the Baath Party. The Council sits in three regular sessions annually but may be called into special session. In theory, the functions of the council include the nomination of a presidential candidate, enactment of laws, discussion of government policy, approval of general budget and development plans, and ratification of treaties. In practice, however, the legislature has no independent authority, because the executive branch effectively controls the legislative process. The assembly may criticize government policies and modify draft laws, but it cannot initiative legislation.

The judicial branch includes courts at three levels: courts of first instance (magistrate courts, summary courts, and peace courts), courts of appeal (one per province), and the Court of Cassation in Damascus, which serves as the highest court of appeal with the authority to resolve both jurisdictional and judicial issues. The Supreme Constitutional Court adjudicates electoral disputes and rules on the constitutionality of laws and decrees. The High Judicial Council, headed by the president and composed of senior civil judges, appoints, transfers, and dismisses judges.

Specialized courts exist outside of the basic three-tiered structure. State security courts, topped by the Supreme State Security Court, hear cases related to national security. In these courts, judgments are not subject to appeal, the president must approve the verdict, and the court is not bound by the same procedures as the courts of regular jurisdiction. Operating under a state of emergency, these special courts do not observe constitutional provisions that safeguard defendants' rights. Military courts can try both military personnel and civilians. There are reports that the government operates military field courts outside established courtrooms, observing fewer of the formal procedures. Economic security courts, which formerly handled economic crimes, were abolished in 2004. Personal status courts deal with matters such as marriage and divorce and are divided along religious lines.

Administrative Divisions: Syria has 14 provinces (*muhafazat*; pl., *muhafazah*): Halab, Dimashq, Dar'a, Rif Dimashq, Dayr az Zawr, Hamah, Al Hasakah, Hims, Idlib, Al Ladhiqiyah, Al Qunaytirah (includes the Golan Heights), Ar Raqqah, As Suwayda, and Tartus. Syrian maps also include the Turkish province of Hatay (Iskenderun). Damascus (Dimashq), Syria's capital, was designated as a province in 1987.

Provincial and Local Government: In practice, government remains highly centralized in Damascus, and provincial governments have little autonomy. Governors, nominated by the minister of interior, approved by the cabinet, and appointed by the central government, head provinces. A provincial council assists each governor. Three-quarters of council members are popularly elected for a term of four years; the minister of interior and the governor appoint the remaining members. Each council has an executive arm consisting of six to 10 officers appointed by the central government from among the council's elected members, each of whom is charged with specific functions. Each province is divided into districts, which, in turn, are divided into sub-districts. Officials appointed by the governor administer districts and sub-districts. These officials serve as intermediaries between central government authority and traditional local leaders, such as village chiefs, clan elders, and councils of elders.

Legal System: Syria's legal system is a mix of Ottoman- and French-based civil law, as well as Islamic law. The constitution requires that Islamic jurisprudence be a main source of legislation. Personal status issues, such as marriage, divorce, paternity, child custody, and inheritance, are governed primarily by customary, Islamic, and other religious laws relating to specific religious communities, with some more recent personal code modifications regarding the status of women, for example. Trials are public (except for juveniles and sex offenses), but Syria does not have trial by jury in regular courts; judges render verdicts. Defendants are entitled to legal representation and to the presumption of innocence, and they are allowed to present evidence and to confront their accusers. Verdicts can be appealed to provincial appeals courts and ultimately to the Court of Cassation.

Electoral System: Syria has universal suffrage at age 18. Direct popular elections are held for president, the National Assembly, and provincial assemblies. In practice, however, the selection of the president is not open to popular choice. Presidential candidates nominated by the Baath Party run unopposed in popular referenda rather than in open elections. The most recent presidential election took place in 2000; the next is due in 2007. The most recent legislative elections occurred in March 2003 and will next take place in 2007.

Politics/Political Parties: Syria is essentially a one-party state, dominated by the Arab Socialist Resurrection (Baath) Party (hereafter, Baath Party). The umbrella National Progressive Front (NPF) encompasses the Baath Party and eight (increased from the original six) allied parties, giving the appearance of a multi-party system. But the NPF has little power independent of the Baath Party. A limited number of independent non-NPF candidates may run for seats in parliament, but the current allotment is set at 83, or 33 percent of seats, based on the 2003 elections, thus ensuring an NPF, and consequently a Baath, majority. In practice, non-Baath parties and independents have little real influence.

Baath Party institutions are parallel to and integrated with Syria's governmental structure. Baath Party members in key positions control the executive and legislative branches of the Syrian government. The Baath party is dominated by the military, which consumes a large share of economic resources. Every four years, the party branches elect representatives to the Party Congress, which then elects the members of the party institutions; the Central Committee has 90 members, and the Regional Command has 21 members. The Regional Command is the highest body of the party and of the state in Syria. The presidential candidate must gain the approval of the Regional Command before being nominated to run for office. The party is headed by a secretary general, a position held by both Hafiz al Asad and his son and successor, Bashar. The National Command is the pan-Arab institution above the Regional Command. The Syrian faction (versus the Iraqi faction) controls most of the Baath Parties of the Arab world.

Mass Media: The constitution guarantees the right to a free press and freedom of expression, but Syria has been functioning under a highly restrictive state of emergency since the Baath Party came to power in 1963. Articles issued under the state of emergency authorize the state to control newspapers, books, radio and television broadcasting, advertising, and the visual arts; and the state retains the right to confiscate and destroy any work that threatens the security of the state. The Syrian government historically has not tolerated independent sources of information. The media are state-owned and controlled by the Baath Party through the office of the Ministry of Information. Media workers are government employees, and a high position requires loyal party membership. Passed in the wake of the Damascus Spring, the provisions of Decree No. 50 of 2001, applying to publishers, editors, journalists, authors, printers, distributors and bookstore owners, make most publications state-owned. Anyone wishing to establish an independent paper or periodical must apply for a license from the Ministry of Information.

Criticism of the president and his family, the ruling Baath Party, and the military is forbidden. The legitimacy of the regime may not be questioned. The government's human rights record, Islamist opposition, allegations of official involvement in drug trafficking, the activity of Syrian troops in Lebanon, and anything unfavorable to the Arab cause in the Arab-Israeli conflict are topics that are usually censored. The government monitors domestic radio and television news broadcasts to ensure adherence to government policies, although foreign broadcasts are not censored, and satellite dishes are available and widely used. The government also screens and blocks access to Internet sites that are regarded as politically sensitive or pornographic. Human rights groups have documented cases of arrest, expulsion, mistreatment, harassment, and assassination of prominent journalists. Nevertheless, the government has not succeeded in maintaining total control. The public does have access to Western radio stations and satellite TV, and al Jazeera has become very popular in Syria.

Foreign Relations: The Arab-Israeli conflict remains the paramount foreign policy concern for Syria, with the Syrian objective of securing withdrawal of Israeli forces from the occupied territories and restoring sovereignty over the Israeli-annexed Golan Heights. Relations with Egypt, Jordan, and the Palestinian Authority have been marked by antipathy since Egypt and Jordan signed separate peace treaties with Israel. However, since the breakdown of the Israeli-Palestinian peace process in 2000, Syria's relations with all three have improved, and Syria continues to seek to play an active pan-Arab role. Syrian-Israeli relations also spill over into Lebanon's national security and internal political structure. Syria has maintained military forces and intelligence personnel in Lebanon since the beginning of the Lebanese civil war in 1976, a situation that further complicates the Arab-Israeli peace process. In early 2005, Syria was under strong international pressure to begin withdrawing its forces from Lebanon and reportedly agreed to do so by the end of April.

Syria's relations with Iraq historically have been characterized by rivalry and conflict. Syria sided with Iran during the Iran-Iraq War (1980–88), which led to a severe breakdown in relations with Iraq. In 1990 Syria participated in the United States-led multinational coalition against Iraq in the 1991 Gulf War. In 1998, primarily for economic reasons, Syria sought improved relations with Iraq, reopening the border and resuming trade. Syria opposed the U.S.-led invasion of Iraq in 2003 and since then has been accused of aiding the insurgency in Iraq. However, according to the U.S. Department of State, Syria pledged qualified support for the Interim Iraqi Government as well as Iraqi elections in early 2005, in the interest of regional stability.

Throughout the Cold War, Syria was within the Soviet sphere of influence, and received strong military support from Russia, but the collapse of the Soviet Union in 1991 initiated an improvement in ties with the West. For example, Syria joined the U.S.-led alliance against Iraq in the Gulf War. This cooperation brought better political and economic relations with the United States, the European Union, and oil-rich Arab states. However, Syria remains on the U.S. list of states "sponsoring terrorism," and relations between Syria and the United States have been especially tense since September 11, 2001, even though Syria has engaged in limited cooperation with the United States in the global war on terrorism. In late 2003, the U.S. Congress passed the Syria Accountability and Lebanese Sovereignty Restoration Act authorizing the imposition of certain sanctions if Syria did not withdraw its forces from Lebanon and stop supporting terrorism, seeking weapons of mass destruction, and aiding the insurgency in Iraq. In mid-2004, President Bush determined that Syria had not met these conditions and implemented sanctions.

Membership in International Organizations: Syria is a member of the Arab Bank for Economic Development in Africa, Arab Fund for Economic and Social Development, Arab Monetary Fund, Council of Arab Economic Unity, Economic and Social Commission for Western Asia, Food and Agriculture Organization of the United Nations, Group of 24, Group of 77, International Atomic Energy Agency, International Bank for Reconstruction and Development, International Chamber of Commerce, International Civil Aviation Organization, International Criminal Police Organization, International Development Association, International Finance Corporation, International Fund for Agricultural Development, International Labour Organization, International Maritime Organization, International Monetary Fund, International Olympic Committee, International Telecommunication Union, Islamic Development Bank, League of Arab States, League of Red Cross and Red Crescent Societies, Non-Aligned Movement, Organization of Arab Petroleum Exporting Countries, Organization of the Islamic Conference, United Nations, UN Conference on Trade and Development, UN Industrial Development Organization, UN Relief and Works Agency for Palestine Refugees in the Near East, Universal Postal Union, World Federation of Trade Unions, World Health Organization, World Meteorological Organization, and World Tourism Organization.

Major International Treaties: Syria is a signatory to a number of international environmental treaties, including those on Biodiversity, Climate Change, Desertification, Endangered Species, Hazardous Wastes, Ozone Layer Protection, Ship Pollution, and Wetlands. It has signed but not ratified a convention on Environmental Modification. Syria is also a party to the Geneva Conventions, Nuclear Test Ban Treaty, Treaty on the Non-Proliferation of Nuclear Weapons, and about half of the international conventions on terrorism. It is not a party to the international convention banning chemical weapons; it has signed but not ratified the biological weapons convention.

NATIONAL SECURITY

Armed Forces Overview: Syria's armed forces include an army, navy, air force, and air defense forces, with a total of 296,800 active personnel and 354,000 reserves (up to age 45) in 2004. The army had 200,000 active personnel and 280,000 reserves; the navy, 7,600 active personnel and 4,000 reserves; the air force, 35,000 active personnel and 70,000 reserves; and the Air Defence

Command, 54,200 active personnel. In the past, Syria was highly dependent on Soviet military training, matériel, and aid/credit. The fall of the Soviet Union deprived Syria of this vital support and has hampered Syria's ability to modernize its arsenal. Nevertheless, Syria's military is regarded as one of the largest and most capable in the Middle East.

Foreign Military Relations: Traditionally, Syria's primary military alliance was with the Soviet bloc, and arms transfers, training, and other military assistance from Russia and other former Soviet states have continued. Syria also is believed to have engaged in military cooperation with Iran, China, and North Korea. Following the Gulf War, Syria was rewarded for its participation on the side of the coalition with substantial financial aid from Gulf Arab states, a large portion of which was devoted to military spending. In 2002 Syria reportedly signed a military cooperation agreement with Turkey, although the relations between the two states are often tense because of their dispute over water from the Euphrates River and alleged Syrian support for Kurdish guerrillas in Turkey.

External Threat: Syria regards Israel as its principal enemy and has long sought to achieve strategic parity with Israel in order to defend its national security and recover the Golan Heights, seized by Israel in 1967. Iraq has long been an ideological and political rival within the Baath movement, and Syria supported Iran in the Iran-Iraq War (1980–88). Since the U.S.-led invasion of Iraq in 2003, Syria has been threatened by the spillover of refugees and violence from Iraq as well as the possibility of U.S. military action directed at Syria. To its west, Syria perceives as a threat the emergence in Lebanon of either a radical Muslim state or a Christian-dominated state aligned with Israel. As a result, Syria has sought to control Lebanese affairs and has stationed military forces there since October 1976, ostensibly as a peacekeeping force.

Defense Budget: In 2003 Syria's defense expenditures reportedly totaled about US$1.5 billion, or 7 percent of the country's gross domestic product (GDP), as compared with US$1.1 billion in 2001 and US$1.2 billion in 2002.

Major Military Units: Syria's ground forces are organized into three corps with a total of 12 divisions (seven armored, three mechanized, one Republican Guard, and one Special Forces). In addition, the army has four independent infantry brigades, one Border Guard brigade, two independent artillery brigades, two independent antitank brigades, 10 independent Special Forces regiments, three surface-to-surface missile (SSM) brigades, and two coastal defense SSM brigades. The navy operates from three bases, at Latakia, Minet el Baida, and Tartus. The air force has nine fighter/ground-attack squadrons and 16 fighter squadrons. The Air Defence Command is organized in two air defense divisions with 25 air defense brigades and two surface-to-air missile regiments.

Major Military Equipment: The army is equipped with 4,600 main battle tanks (1,200 of which are in static positions or storage), 800 reconnaissance vehicles, 2,100 armored infantry fighting vehicles, 1,600 armored personnel carriers, 1,630 towed artillery pieces, 430 self-propelled artillery pieces, 480 multiple rocket launchers, 710 mortars, 72 surface-to-surface missile (SSM) launchers and about 850 SSM missiles, 4,190 antitank guided weapons, an unspecified number of rocket launchers, 2,050 air defense guns, and 4,335 surface-to-air missiles (SAMs). The navy is equipped with two frigates, 12 missile craft, 8 inshore patrol craft, 5 mine countermeasure ships, 3 amphibious ships, and 4 support and miscellaneous ships. Naval aviation resources include 16 armed helicopters. The air force is equipped with 520 combat aircraft and 71 armed helicopters (including some in storage). Air defense forces are endowed with 160 SAM batteries and more than 828 surface-to-air missiles as well as 4,000 air defense artillery pieces.

Syria seeks both to sustain its conventional forces and to develop weapons of mass destruction (WMD). In January 2004, Syria appeared to have tacitly admitted to possession of WMD when Assad stated that Syria would only agree to dismantle its WMD if Israel did the same.

Military Service: Syria has a 30-month period of compulsory military service for males, who become eligible for conscription at age 18. In 2004 available males aged 15–49 totaled an estimated 4.9 million. Those judged fit for service totaled 2.7 million. Approximately 216,000 males reach the age of conscription annually.

Paramilitary Forces: Syria's paramilitary forces comprise the Gendarmerie, administered by the Ministry of Interior, which has 8,000 regular personnel, and the Workers' Militia, or People's Army, operated by the Baath Party, with an estimated 100,000 reserves.

Foreign Military Forces: The United Nations has 1,029 troops stationed in Syria with contingents from Austria (364), Canada (186), Japan (30), Nepal (1), Poland (356), and Slovakia (92). Russia has about 150 advisers in Syria, primarily for air defense purposes.

Military Forces Abroad: At least 16,000 Syrian troops have been deployed in Lebanon since October 1976, forming one mechanized division, with elements of one armored and four mechanized infantry brigades, as well as elements of 10 Special Forces and two artillery regiments. In early 2005, Syria was subjected to strong U.S. and international pressure to withdraw its forces from Lebanon following the assassination of the Lebanese prime minister, an act of terrorism in which Syria was suspected by many of complicity or at least indirect involvement. At the end of March, Syria reportedly had moved some troops back across the border and redeployed others in eastern Lebanon. In early April, Syria announced that it would complete the withdrawl of its military forces and intelligence personnel by the end of the month.

Police: Security services play a powerful role in Syrian society, monitoring and repressing opposition to the regime. The internal security apparatus is large and effective, with several security services that operate independently of each other and of the law, including the Political Security Directorate (PSD), Syrian Military Intelligence (SMI), General Intelligence Directorate (GID), and Air Force Security (AFS). Only the PSD, subordinate to the Ministry of Interior, is under civilian control. Human rights violations are common. Police forces, under the Ministry of Interior, consist of four separate forces: emergency police, local neighborhood police, riot police, and traffic police.

Internal Threat: Repression of internal dissent is effective, and public criticism of the regime is generally muted and circumspect. Sectarian rivalry within Syria's many religious and ethnic communities has been a perennial source of instability, in particular resentment of the well-connected Alawi. The regime systematically represses the Kurdish minority, fearing any push for

Kurdish autonomy. In March 2004, Kurdish riots erupted in Al Hasakah Province and then spread to other parts of the country. Security forces reportedly killed more than 30 persons and arrested more than 11,000. The regime also fears a resurgence of Sunni Islamic fundamentalists. Security forces reportedly conducted mass arrests of suspected Islamists and Muslim Brotherhood adherents throughout 2004. Given Syria's long history of military coups and countercoups prior to the Assad regime, the possibility of a military coup may also constitute a potential threat to Syrian stability.

Terrorism: Syria has publicly condemned terrorism, but the government makes a distinction between terrorism and what it views as legitimate resistance against Israel. As such, Syria continues to support the Lebanon-based Hezbollah, a Shiite Muslim group, as well as the Palestinian group, Hamas. The Popular Front for the Liberation of Palestine-General Command (PFLP-GC) is based in Damascus. Syria has cooperated with the United States and others against al Qaeda and the Taliban. Nevertheless, in 2004 the United States accused Syria of permitting, if not actively facilitating, the movement of funds and insurgents into Iraq. In mid-2004, in accordance with the Syria Accountability Act passed by the U.S. Congress in December 2003, the United States imposed economic sanctions on Syria because of Syria's support for terrorism, continued occupation of Lebanon, pursuit of weapons of mass destruction and missile programs, and efforts to undermine stabilization and reconstruction in Iraq.

Human Rights: According to the U.S. Department of State's 2004 report on human rights, Syria's human rights record remains poor. A state of emergency has been in effect since 1963. Security forces continue to commit numerous and serious human rights abuses including arbitrary arrest and detention, torture in detention, prolonged detention without trial, fundamentally unfair trials in the security courts, and infringement on privacy rights. Police and security forces are corrupt. Prison conditions are poor and do not meet international standards for health and sanitation. The regime significantly restricts freedom of speech, press, assembly, and association and imposes some limits on freedom of religion and freedom of movement. Kurds suffer systematic discrimination. After a brief period in 2000–2001 known as Damascus Spring, during which time independent debating clubs were established, satellite dishes became much more prominent, Internet cafés opened, new independent print publications were established, and political detainees from across the political spectrum were released, Decree No. 50/2001 was passed, which places severe restrictions on the media, especially the print media. According to Arab Press Freedom Watch, the current regime has one of the worst records on freedom of expression in the Arab world.